More Encouraging
Stories to Help You

KEEP
ON
KEEPING
ON *With Jesus*

Also by Jim Gilley:

The Battle Is the Lord's

Fake News

God for Us

God With Us

Keep On Keeping On

More Encouraging
Stories to Help You

KEEP ON KEEPING ON *With Jesus*

JIM GILLEY

Pacific Press®
Publishing Association
Nampa, Idaho | www.pacificpress.com

Cover design by Gerald Lee Monks
Cover design resources from iStockphoto.com | sezer66
Inside design by Aaron Troia

Copyright © 2020 by Pacific Press® Publishing Association
Printed in the United States of America
All rights reserved

All Scripture quotations are from the New King James Version®. Copyright © 1982 by
Thomas Nelson. Used by permission. All rights reserved.

The author assumes full responsibility for the accuracy of all facts and quotations
as cited in this book.

Purchase additional copies of this book by calling toll-free 1-800-765-6955
or by visiting AdventistBookCenter.com.

ISBN: 978-0-8163-6634-7

February 2020

DEDICATION

God has blessed me with many loyal family members and friends who are like family. Two of these are Gary Grimes and Max Trevino. They have always been there for me! I met both while in high school, and we have been close ever since!

CONTENTS

Chapter One

PREACH THE WORD

During my ministry, I have prepared and preached many hundreds of sermons—to college students, church members in the pew, church administrators, and the general public. But of those many sermons, only one continues to get the same response. Over and over again, listeners have told me, "Pastor, that message came at a critical time in my life, and what a difference it made!" That sermon is titled "Keep On Keeping On."

The greatest problem in people's lives that I have observed over the years is discouragement—people giving up! Life is difficult. You will lose loved ones; you will have setbacks and disappointments; friends will let you down. The message of that sermon is simple: keep on keeping on with Jesus!

The temptation to give up haunted me in my early years of marriage, ministry, and life in general. Then God, through the Holy Spirit, let me have a glimpse of Jesus and the pain, rejection, and betrayal He suffered. But even though that rejection nailed Him to a cross, Jesus never quit. He refused to give up on His mission to save everyone who would accept Him.

The version of "Keep On Keeping On" that you will be

reading in this book was preached a number of years ago at the Florida camp meeting. In the audience that night was Medal of Honor recipient Desmond Doss. I couldn't help thinking about how Doss was persecuted for his faith by some of the same men he saved at Hacksaw Ridge! He was determined to keep on keeping on until every injured soldier was rescued.

I have had the privilege to sit at the feet, so to speak, of some great teachers and preachers—Fordyce Detamore, Dick Barron (who was later killed in a tragic plane crash), H. M. S. Richards Sr. and Jr., Don Jacobson, E. E. Cleveland, C. D. Brooks, and Charles Bradford, to name a few! I've had great teachers such as M. D. Lewis, Ivan Blazen, E. R. Thiele, Edward Heppenstal, and others. While I was at the seminary, Dr. Edward Banks challenged us to study some of the outstanding Protestant ministers, not for their theology but for their ability to communicate through preaching. We studied the sermons of Billy Graham, Norman Vincent Peale, Charles Swindoll, W. A. Criswell, John MacArthur, and Lloyd John Ogilvie. I was blessed by some more than others, and was often confounded by the fact that these sincere men of God could not understand the fourth commandment the way Seventh-day Adventists do!

My most exciting years of preaching were the seven years during which I had the privilege of being the senior pastor of the Arlington, Texas, Seventh-day Adventist church. For five of those years, I was joined by Henry Barron, my mentor and friend. I pastored there for one dollar per year!

During most of those years, I was also vice president of L. H. Coleman's stewardship organization. My normal schedule was to go into my study on Sunday morning to copy chapters from books on the subject I was preparing for next Sabbath's sermon. I would build a file folder with chapters on that subject. Also, in that file folder, I would put several sheets of paper on which I jotted down thoughts while I studied. Then on Monday, I would usually fly to a location where I would be working with local church leadership, training and organizing individuals into teams to inspire their fellow church members to support the Coleman Stewardship Program.

When I had a few minutes, I would study. On Thursday, I would fly back to Dallas, finalizing my sermon notes on the flight. Friday morning, I would give my notes to Kathy Smith, the secretary at Coleman Stewardship, who would type them for me.

Friday night and Sabbath morning, I would immerse myself in the message, jotting a few keywords in the margin of my Bible. Then I would leave the notes in my briefcase, trusting the Holy Spirit to bring to my lips the words I should present.

I started preaching without notes quite by accident during my first pastorate—or perhaps by divine intervention. As an intern pastor, I held a Week of Prayer at Pioneer Valley Academy in Massachusetts. I was young and connected with the kids. They invited me to come back and be the Friday night speaker at their graduation—the first graduating class in the new school's history.

I studied hard all week and wrote my sermon out in a manuscript. I typed it myself and put it in a folder. When I arrived at the school a few minutes before the service was to begin, I reached into the back seat of the car for the folder—and it wasn't there! I was scared to death anyway, but now I was sick. I ran to the bathroom. In the stall, I jotted down a few keywords. There was no time left, so I went on the platform. In the audience were two men from the General Conference who had children graduating that day. One of them should have been speaking, but here I was—without a sermon!

Do you know what happened? The Holy Spirit brought every point to my mind! I had the freedom to connect with the audience, and God blessed abundantly.

The president of the local conference, Elder Merle Mills, was sitting next to me, and I tried to hide the fact that I didn't have notes! Later I heard that he had remarked about how impressed he was that a young preacher would preach without notes.

It takes a lot more preparation time to preach without notes. But the freedom to truly communicate the message makes it worth the time it takes.

It also takes a lot of help for us to get a book into a readable condition. My wife, Camille, and now adult children, Jim Jr., Maryann, John, and Amy, have always been so encouraging and supportive. Kathy Smith has always been there to type the manuscripts. Her ability to decipher my handwriting amazes me. Dale Galusha, Pacific Press president, has encouraged me to write and has been there since my first book. Russ Holt, the most talented re-write genius, smoothes out my rough sentences but still makes it sound like me. Thank you, Russ, and of course, there are many others.

So many of these messages were inspired by other preachers of the Word. If I haven't given proper credit, I apologize.

Preach the Word, and keep on keeping on!

Chapter Two

KEEP
ON
KEEPING
ON

℘

"He who endures to the end shall be saved."
—Mark 13:13

In 1954, Jim Peters ran the twenty-six-mile marathon in the Canada Games. At that time, Peters was the greatest marathoner in the world. Marathons had just come back into their own, but they were nothing like the marathons of today that have seventeen thousand or eighteen thousand runners in a race, such as the Boston Marathon. When the contestants come down to the end, there will be a huge group running all together just seconds apart right at the end of the line. But in 1954, Jim Peters was the man to beat. When the officials fired the starting gun, Peters started sprinting out ahead of everybody else. And he stayed there until right near the end. In fact, as Jim Peters entered the arena marking the end of the race, he was fifteen minutes ahead of the person in second place—a Scotsman by the name of Joe McGhee. A fifteen-minute lead!

Now a couple of great things had already happened that day. If you've seen me, you can tell that I'm not a track star! But I have read a little bit about track, and I followed track events back in those days. I used to tell people that I wanted to be a jockey because when I was young and small, I loved horses. I thought being a jockey would be great, but I'm definitely not qualified to be a jockey anymore! Today, I'm more like the guy who said, "I always thought I'd like to run in the Kentucky Derby, but unfortunately, I'd have a better chance now as a horse than I would as a jockey!"

As Peters entered the arena, the eighty thousand spectators were as excited as they could be because something historic had happened only moments before. The one-mile race had just taken place, and Dr. Roger Bannister had run that mile in under four minutes! There had never been anyone who had broken the four-minute mile before that time. In fact, the experts and those who supposedly knew about such things said it couldn't be done—that someone would ever run a mile in four minutes or less.

And that wasn't all. Right behind Bannister was John Landy. Both men finished the mile that day in under four minutes! The crowd had seen a record broken. Now they were about to see another record broken—this one for the twenty-six-mile marathon.

As Jim Peters entered that arena, the crowd was already charged up from what they had just seen. They stood to their feet—all eighty thousand of them—and were applauding Jim Peters. Then suddenly, Peters fell, and the crowd gasped. He hadn't crossed the finish line! There was nothing the crowd could do for him. According to the rules, you cannot help somebody; you cannot pick them up and help them across the finish line.

The crowd shouted words of encouragement, but to no avail. A number of articles have been written about what happened next. If you want to read about this, look up "Jim Peters" on the internet. One account says that the next fifteen minutes were horrendous. Peters kept trying to get up and make it to the finish line, yet he kept falling time after time. At last, he was able to get to his feet, but he was disoriented and turned the wrong direction! He fell again, and this time his trainer caught him. Doctors rushed to him, one of which was Dr. Roger Bannister. Seven doctors started working on Jim Peters right there in the arena. They loaded him into an ambulance and took him to a hospital. He was so severely dehydrated he had to stay in the hospital for seven days. He finally recovered, but he never raced again. Jim Peters's days as a marathon runner were through.

Fifteen minutes later, Joe McGhee came running into the arena, went around, crossed the finish line, and was crowned the victor. Then another runner came in, and another, and another. But Jim Peters lost the race. Why? Because he didn't finish. The Bible says, "He who endures to the end shall be saved" (Mark 13:13). Running most of the course is not good enough. Trusting Jesus most of the way is not good enough. We've got to trust Him *all* the way because we don't win the race of life in our own strength. We win in *His* strength, *His* power.

Life isn't always easy. Jesus warned His followers, "You will be hated by all for My name's sake. But he who endures to the end shall be saved" (Mark 13:13).

The Savior promises to be with us and give us His power to overcome, but He doesn't promise that the Christian life will always be easy. In fact, there are numerous texts in the

Bible pointing out that the devil is going to make it as hard as he can on Christians and that we need to persevere.

Jesus says to the early Christian church, "Do not fear any of those things which you are about to suffer. Indeed, the devil is about to throw some of you into prison, that you may be tested. . . . Be faithful until death, and I will give you the crown of life" (Revelation 2:10).

So Jesus has a crown for you. "Be faithful," He urges. "Hold on to it; it's yours. Don't give it up. I will help you and keep you, but you need to keep on keeping on." He continues, "Because you have kept My command to persevere, I also will keep you from the hour of trial which shall come upon the whole world" (Revelation 3:10).

There it is again—"persevere." "Be faithful." Endure to the end. If you keep on keeping on, you will receive the crown of life that Jesus has reserved for you. I believe that Jesus is coming soon. I believe it with all of my heart. And I believe that He is going to see to it that every single one of us who wants to be saved, who wants to be in the kingdom, is going to be there—if we continue to trust in Him. It's when we step aside, when we give up on Jesus, that we forfeit the crown of life that Jesus promises to give us. Don't give up on Him! Don't give away your crown!

Let's face it. We still live in a world of sin and pain and suffering. Life isn't always easy. Some people reading this book may have a terminal disease. Your marriage may be falling apart. Your children may have turned away from God and the church they once knew. There is hurt and pain everywhere we look in this old world. But, you know, Jesus promises, *"I will never leave you nor forsake you"* (Hebrews 13:5; emphasis added). Jesus is the only One who can heal that pain. He's the only One who can bring you through the difficulties of this world. And He will keep His promise to stand beside you, no matter what you're facing. But you've got to hang in there and trust Him. You've got to keep on keeping on.

Somebody has written a little poem that goes like this:

> It takes a little courage,
> And a little self-control,
> And a grim determination,
> If you want to reach the goal.
>
> It takes a deal of striving,
> And a firm and stern-set chin,
> No matter what the battle,
> If you really want to win.
>
> There's no easy path to glory;
> There is no road to fame.
> Life, however we may view it,
> Is no simple parlor game.
>
> But its prizes call for fighting,
> For endurance and for grit.
> For a rugged disposition,
> And a "don't know when to quit."
>
> You must take a blow or give one;
> You must risk and you must lose,
> And expect that in the struggle
> That you'll suffer from a bruise.

But you mustn't wince or falter,
If a fight you once begin.
Be a man and face the battle—
That's the only way to win!

The apostle Paul echoes the sentiments of that little poem when he says, "Let us not grow weary while doing good, for in due season we shall reap if we do not lose heart" (Galatians 6:9). And from what I see today, far too many people are losing heart and giving up—giving up on God, giving up on their families, giving up on their children. In these difficult times, we need God more than at any other time in our history; we need Jesus Christ and the power of the Holy Spirit in our lives more than we've ever needed them before. Now is not the time for quitting; this is a time for moving forward and trusting in our Lord and Savior Jesus Christ.

When I was a young man, I went to school at Andrews University in Michigan as an undergraduate student for my last two years of college (the first two years were at Southwestern Junior College, in Keene, Texas). Here I was, a southern boy, and I went up there to the north. Andrews University is located in Berrien Springs, Michigan. I called it "Siberian Springs"! I'd never been through a cold northern winter before, and it was *cold*! It was cold even in March!

In the spring, when there was still snow on the ground, I would get discouraged. Dr. Thiele was my major professor; he was a great man, a great student of God's Word, and a great person. He often told a story to his students, and since I took several classes from him, I heard the story several times. The story was about his uncle who had diabetes. This was before there were medications for diabetes, so his uncle was put on a very restrictive diet. There were only certain things he could eat. He would sit down at the table, and his wife would put in front of him a little plate of what he called his "rabbit food." Then the rest of the family would sit down and have the blessing over mashed potatoes and homemade rolls and corn on the cob and all kinds of good food with dessert afterward—everything he couldn't eat! But he was faithful to this diet for twenty years until one day he finally announced, "I'm going to eat what I want even if it kills me." And he did. And you know what—it did kill him! That's right. They buried him. And two weeks later, injectable insulin came on the market! If he had just waited a little bit longer. "He who endures to the end shall be saved."

Have you ever really wanted to quit? Well, I have—more than once! A number of those experiences took place when I was in college. I remember once winning $125 at the amateur hour program when I was in college in Texas. I had never had so much money in my life. I was on top of the world that Saturday night. But Sunday I crashed. Monday was even worse. And on Tuesday, I walked into the registrar's office and said, "I need a drop voucher."

And the woman there said, "Why do you need a drop voucher?"

"Because I want to drop some classes."

She gave me the form. I had started filling it out when she stopped me. "Wait a minute," she said. "You're dropping *all* of your classes?"

"Yes," I told her.

"If you drop more than two classes," she said, "you have to see President Scales."

"OK," I replied. "Let me see him." So she ushered me into his office.

"You're leaving school?" he asked.

"Yes."

"Why?"

"Because I'm sick of it around here," I told him. "I'm sick of the rules. I'm just sick of this whole place."

Elder Scales looked at me and said, "What's the real reason that you're going to quit?"

"Well," I replied, "I don't like the food here. I don't like all the restrictions."

He said, "You've been here a while. You know how to handle all that stuff. What's the real reason?"

"I'm behind on my bill."

"You've been behind on your bill ever since you got here," he said. "What's the real reason?"

"Well," I replied, "My grades aren't as good as I'd like them to be."

He smiled. "Your grades have never been all that great." Then he looked at me, and he said, "Is it because you've broken up with your girlfriend?"

And I blurted out, "How did you know?"

He said, "Everybody knows!"

Wow! That made it even worse! I wanted to leave for sure now.

I said, "President Scales, I can't even eat. I can't stand to see her. I get sick, physically sick when I see her."

She and I had signed up for several classes together. On the first day of class, you sit beside the persons you want to sit with, and the teacher makes out a seating chart, and you sit in that spot from then on. I sat beside her in every class we had together. We were lab partners in biology class, cutting up frogs together!

"I can't take it," I told the president. "I've got to get out of here. Please, just sign the form. I have to leave."

He said, "Gilley, I'm going to leave this form right here on my desk. I want you to go over to the dorm, pack a bag, and get out of here. Don't take all of your clothes—just a small bag. I'm not going to ask you where you're going, but when you come back here next Monday, I'll sign this form if you tell me you still want me to. I'll even date it with today's date." (He knew I was worried about my bill getting larger and larger, you see.) "You don't have to go home; I don't care where you go. But be back here on Monday morning. And take care of yourself."

I hitchhiked out of town and ended up in some small town. I went into a little café. I had that $125 in my pocket from the amateur hour. I hadn't been eating and had lost fifteen pounds. In those days, I weighed only 150 pounds and couldn't afford to lose fifteen of them. I sat down at the counter of that little diner and ordered something to eat. When the food came, I tried to eat, but I couldn't. It was making me feel sick.

They call it "puppy love," you know. But it's real to the puppy! I've conducted funerals for three suicides, and two of them were over girls. Puppy love can be a serious thing. Don't turn your back on a lovesick kid.

As I was sitting there playing with my food, the waitress came by. She looked at me and said, "You'll get over her."

I said, "What?"

She said, "You've broken up with your girlfriend."

"How did you know?" I asked.

"It's written all over your face," she said.

I got out of there right away and went to east Texas, where my brother Ed lived, and spent some days with him. I read some Scripture. We played some golf—my brother played well; I didn't, but I enjoyed being with him. I read some philosophy and finally was able to eat and get my strength back.

On Monday morning, I walked into President Scales's office and told him, "You can tear up that drop voucher because if anybody's going to leave this campus, it's her!"

And I set out to be as mean and ornery to that poor girl as I could possibly be. I wouldn't have given her the time of day if she'd have begged me to. Now, you and I understand that is a classic defense mechanism, right? I decided I would absolutely show her no attention at all. That girl meant a lot to me, and she still does. We got together a year later, and Camille and I have been together over forty years now!

So many times I've wondered to myself what would have happened if President Scales had said to me, "Good riddance, Gilley. You've been nothing but a pain since you've been here." He would have been telling the truth. But instead, he was into saving people and encouraging people, and he saved me. He encouraged me at a time when I needed it. What would have happened if he had written me off? Camille and I have four beautiful children and six beautiful grandchildren!

I believe there are times in life when you shouldn't make a decision. There are times in life when you should just trust in God and not do anything. Don't go forward; don't go backward; don't go any direction at all until you come to your senses—and then the Lord will lead you. The Bible says, "A righteous man may fall seven times and rise again, but the wicked shall fall by calamity" (Proverbs 24:16). The only difference between the righteous man who falls and the wicked man who falls is that the righteous man gets back up! And he is able to keep on getting back up because he doesn't depend on himself. He depends on Jesus, and he gets back up by the grace of Jesus Christ. The wicked man stays down.

Peter and Judas both denied Christ. What a tremendous story it would have been if Judas had come back and confessed his sin to Jesus! Wow, what a story! And that could have happened, but Judas gave up on Jesus. Judas made a tragic, *tragic* mistake. Peter denied the Lord too. He denied Him vehemently with cursing and swearing, but Peter got back up; he came back to the Lord. And what a difference that made in his life!

There have been so many times in my life when I have felt like giving up. When Camille and I were first in the ministry and our son Jimmy was a baby, we got one of our first paychecks. After we paid our tithe and our bills, we had eight dollars left to buy food, formula for the baby, gas—everything else for the rest of the month. Now, that's a lot of month left for eight dollars to cover! We were discouraged. "Lord," we complained, "is this how You want us to live? How can we do this?"

Now, we had determined we were going to pay tithe no matter what, so we went ahead and did that. But we were wondering, "Lord, how can we make it?" The first thing we did was to get in the car and go for a drive. We should have been saving our gasoline, but we couldn't think of anything else to do right then. So we went driving around. When we returned home, someone was sitting out in front of our house. His name was Howard Lee. "Could you guys use some food?" he asked. In those days, Howard was the representative for Worthington Foods in that area.

Could we use some food? We really didn't have any food in the house to speak of.

Howard said, "I've got a whole lot of these samples, and I want you to take them and use them and encourage people in your district to buy some of these new frozen foods." He started unloading a whole bunch of this stuff and brought it into our house.

And Camille and I said, "Thank You, Lord. You are seeing us through a difficult time." Hang on to Jesus! Keep on keeping on. Trust in Him, because He will see you through. "He who endures to the end shall be saved."

One of the most difficult experiences of my college life was Greek class. No one in my family had ever taken any language in school other than English. In Greek class, it was all Greek to me!

My wife was going to school. I was going to school. I was taking a full load of classes and also running a little business that I'd started. I was trying to keep everything going and having a very difficult time doing so. I didn't have four hours a day to put into Greek.

One day, our teacher came into Greek class and said, "Last night, I was driving along the Ohio Turnpike when I heard a preacher on the radio. At the end of his sermon, he said something that he said was a motto of his, and it's going to be the motto for this class as well. This is what he said: 'Keep on keeping on.' "

The teacher wrote that phrase on the board. I wrote it in my Greek textbook. Then the teacher said, "If you keep coming to class and keep trying, I promise you that you're going to make it." That was the first ray of hope I'd had in that class, and I suspect it was the same for a number of my classmates.

Whenever I tell that story, my kids—who have all been great students—tell me, "Dad, don't tell that story! People think stupidity is hereditary, and they'll think we've got it too! Please don't tell that story!"

But I remember when it was time for the grades to come out. I wasn't worried about any of my classes except Greek class. I had done all right in the others, but I was concerned about Greek. Several of us were standing in line to get our final grades. There was a big, tall fellow standing in front of me, who was so nervous he couldn't hide it. He said, "Gilley, I am really concerned."

And I said, "What are you concerned about?"

"I'm concerned," he said, "because from the first grade until now, I've gotten straight As—nothing else. But I'm concerned I might have slipped to a B in Greek!"

And I replied, "Wow! You really do have a problem!"

I didn't tell him I was worried too. Well, when this fellow got his grades, he jumped up and nearly hit the ceiling. "Whoopee!" he yelled. "Straight As!" And he took off down the hall.

Then it was my turn. I walked up and gave my name, and the person handed me my grades. I was looking for only one; I knew the others were OK. I ran down the list quickly, looking for my grade in Greek class. When I saw it, I jumped up and nearly hit the ceiling myself. "Whoopee!" I yelled. "I got a D!"

Keep on keeping on! Keep on holding on to Jesus. Keep

on trusting in Him, because He is going to see you through. "He who endures to the end shall be saved."

When you look at Jacob in the Old Testament, what kind of person was he? Jacob was a thief and a deceiver. But he wrestled with God and wouldn't let go (Genesis 32:22–32). Jacob kept on keeping on. And God changed that thief! Jacob wasn't a young man when God changed his life and changed his name to *Israel*—"overcomer." Throughout the Old Testament, God often refers to Himself as "the God of Jacob." God identified with that former thief and deceiver because he wouldn't give up. Because Jacob kept on keeping on, God changed him and saved him.

It's the same with Moses. Moses was a murderer. He killed a man (Exodus 2:11, 12). A man challenged me once when I made that statement. He said, "Moses wasn't a murderer."

"Don't try to convince the Egyptians that Moses wasn't a murderer," I replied. "Call it whatever you like, but that Egyptian was dead when Moses finished with him."

Moses tried to hide what he had done, but he didn't do a good job of burying the body. Someone found out, and they talked about it, so Moses had to flee the country and go out into the wilderness. It took a long time, but Moses kept on keeping on, and God used him. God used a murderer!

God placed the Ten Commandments in Moses' hands, one of which said, "You shall not murder" (Exodus 20:13). And there was Moses, holding a commandment that said, "You are a murderer, Moses." But God used Moses and changed him, so that centuries later, Moses stood on another mountain, the Mount of Transfiguration, along with Elijah and Jesus—he stood there, a mortal man changed by God. A man who had to spend all that time in the wilderness before

God was able to get through to him. But He did. Moses could have quit somewhere along the line, but Moses kept on trusting in God, kept on holding on to God. And God kept holding on to him, and He saved him.

Then we look at David—a murderer *and* an adulterer! Yet God declared later that David did nothing wrong in His sight (1 Kings 14:8)! God forgot all of David's sins! Why? Because David kept trusting in Him, he kept claiming the blood. When David offered the sacrifice for his sins, he didn't see a lamb; he saw the Messiah to come. He saw the One who was to be the Lamb of God and take away the sin of the world (John 1:29).

We live in a difficult world, and we are moving along toward the end of it. The Bible says, "He who endures to the end shall be saved." When you see someone fall, reach down and lift that person up.

The apostle Paul says, "Brethren, I do not count myself to have apprehended; but one thing I do, forgetting those things which are behind and reaching forward to those things which are ahead, I press toward the goal for the prize of the upward call of God in Christ Jesus" (Philippians 3:13, 14).

Paul tells us to forget those things that are behind us—all those mistakes and sins and sorrows. The devil says, "Don't forget them. Keep them fresh and festering in your mind." And if you do forget them, he'll get someone to come along and remind you of them and drag it all back up again! That's what the devil does.

Paul says, "Forget those things. Reach forward and keep your eyes on the future. Press toward the goal for the prize God has in store for you. Keep on keeping on!" You see, the apostle Paul had a lot to forget. He had persecuted Christians; he had been the one who saw to it that Stephen was stoned. Some of the Christians in Jerusalem loved Stephen so much that they never forgot Paul's role in his death. In fact, I have a feeling they would drag it up every once in a while, because Paul says, "Forgetting those things which are behind and reaching forward to those things which are ahead, I press toward the goal for the prize of the upward call of God in Christ Jesus" (Philippians 3:13, 14).

There was another time in my life when I truly felt like the world was falling in on me. You know, when that happens, you keep hearing this voice in your head, saying, *"Give up."* But remember this: That voice is *never* the voice of God. God will never, ever tell you to give up. You can give up on sin. You can give up on your own power to live the way you know you should live and the way you want to live. But never give up on God. Never give up on life. Never. Never! It's always the devil that urges you to do that. When you hear that voice, know where it's coming from—it's the devil's voice, not God's.

One particular night I was so discouraged. I remember turning on the radio, trying to find something, somewhere, somebody who could be an encouraging voice. I couldn't find H. M. S. Richards, Billy Graham, or anybody else I knew on the radio. Finally, I settled on an old preacher I'd never heard before. And as I listened to him, he had a message for me! God had him say exactly what I needed to hear that night. It was for me! That preacher didn't know it, but God did.

I believe there is probably someone reading these words right now, who is receiving the message that God wants you to read. I don't know who you are, but you do. God knows, and you know. And that's what is important.

That night I knew God was speaking to me through the words of that radio preacher. When he finished his remarks, he said, "And now, until next week, I want to say to you what I say every week: Keep on keeping on!"

I came up off the floor and ran to find my old Greek textbook right there still in my library. I pulled it out because, in my discouragement, I had forgotten the motto I had written on its flyleaf years before. Somehow, I had come across the same radio preacher my Greek teacher had listened to that night when he was driving along the Ohio Turnpike. He was still sending that motto out over the airwaves—"Keep on keeping on." I said, "Oh, thank You, Father. Thank You for that message."

Hold on to Jesus. Don't let anybody knock you out of the way. Don't let anyone discourage you. Sometimes people say, "I can't stay in the church. Look at all the hypocrites and sinners in the church. The church is full of people like that."

They're right—not about leaving the church, but the church *is* full of imperfect people. It's full of people just like you and me.

Let me ask you something. If you found out tomorrow morning that the Mercedes-Benz dealership downtown was giving away, absolutely free, a brand-new Mercedes Benz to the first twenty-five people in line at the dealership, would you get in line? Let's say you rush down there and manage to be number 10 in line. You're standing there feeling pretty good. You're going to get a free car, and not just any car—a Mercedes Benz!

But then you realize that the guy in front of you—number 9—stinks! Absolutely stinks something awful! And the man behind you—number 11—is talking about how he is going to sell the Mercedes-Benz the minute he gets it and buy two Lincolns! He's a hypocrite, standing in the Mercedes-Benz line, yet preferring Lincolns. You look around, and you notice that a lot of the people in line have problems. Would you say, "I'm not staying in this line any longer"? Would you say, "I'm not going to put up with this smelly guy in front of me; I don't have to stand here and smell that"? Would you leave the line because the guy behind you is a hypocrite?

I bet you'd stay there in line. I bet you would.

Listen, we're standing in line for something far more valuable and important than a new car. We cannot even imagine what heaven and eternal life are going to be like. Don't let anybody drive you out of God's church. Don't do it! Don't let it happen. Don't let anybody discourage you. Hang on to Jesus. Trust in His message; trust in the Word, because He is coming soon, and we want to be faithful until He comes. He has promised, "Be faithful until death, and I will give you the crown of life" (Revelation 2:10).

Keep on keeping on in Jesus!

Chapter Three

THE BATTLE IS THE LORD'S

❧

"The LORD does not save with sword and
spear; for the battle is the LORD's."
—*1 Samuel 17:47*

The apostle Paul had a young friend named Timothy whom he thought of as kind of a son—a son in the faith (1 Timothy 1:2). He wrote Timothy two letters that we find in the New Testament. In one of them, Paul wrote the following: "Pursue righteousness, godliness, faith, love, patience, gentleness. Fight the good fight of faith, lay hold on eternal life" (1 Timothy 6:11, 12).

"Fight the good fight of faith." That's an unusual way to express it, don't you think? We don't often think of faith as involving a fight. But it can.

Sometimes faith feels wonderful! God is close, and the sky is bright and glorious. Life is going great! But sometimes faith is just the opposite. Sometimes it's difficult to totally, completely trust in God. When life isn't going well, it can be really difficult to have faith. It can be hard to trust God when your child is in the hospital or when your spouse has left you or when you've lost your job and things are falling apart. That's when it becomes a fight to hang on to your faith. If you've ever experienced that, you know it can be agony.

Earlier in this book, I told you how much I struggled with Greek in college. But sometimes the Greek I learned comes in handy. *Agon* is the Greek word for "fight." It's where we get our English word *agony*. So in Greek, "fight the good fight of faith" becomes "agonize the agony of faith." The apostle Paul realized that it can sometimes be agonizing to hang on to your faith.

I remember one time when I was a young man, and I was very discouraged. It was the summer between my first and second years of college. I was sitting on the campus of Southwestern Junior College in Texas, all alone on a bench, and I was thinking deeply about a lot of things. I had a very strong feeling that I was getting ready to miss out on both this world and the world to come. I loved baseball. I was a fairly good baseball player. In fact, the previous summer, I had signed a contract with the Giants. Afterward, I had wrestled with that decision and finally came to the place where I said, "No, I'm not going to do it because there is absolutely no way I can be a professional baseball player and keep the Sabbath."

But sitting there on that bench on the college campus, I was agonizing over that decision. I was looking at what it meant to be a Christian. I was focusing on all the require-ments, the perfection of life that God calls us to. And I was saying to myself, "I'm going to lose out on playing baseball, and I'm going to lose out on heaven as well because I'm certainly not perfect. I'm not even close enough to discuss being perfect! I'm going to lose out on heaven, and I'm going to lose out on this earth too! It looks like a lose-lose proposition to me."

So I was sitting out there really agonizing about my faith—what it was and what it meant and what I should do. I was wondering, *Am I making the biggest mistake of my life by trying to follow Jesus?*

Just then, Pastor Leon Strickland came by and saw me sitting there all by myself. He was the associate pastor of the Keene College church. He came over and said, "What are you doing sitting here?"

I said, "Well, some of my friends were going to come in for the weekend, but they're not here yet. I'm just sitting here thinking." And I shared some of my thoughts with him.

He looked at me and said, "Have you ever read the book *Christ Our Righteousness*?"

"No. I've never read it—never even heard of it."

"It's a fantastic book," he told me. "It's a compilation of Ellen White statements put together by A. G. Daniells, who was president of the General Conference for twenty-four years." And Pastor Strickland began to share things with me about how Jesus is the One who wins the battles of our lives.

I listened, and I said, "Oh, I wish I could believe what you're saying. This is fabulous! This is good news; it brings hope!"

And he said, "It's true. Get that book."

You know, I got busy, and I did not get the book. The next Friday night, I was back in our little home in Dallas. My mother and younger brother were the only believers in the family. Friday nights at our home, the television would be on, because the rest of the family reserved all television privileges. Our home wasn't necessarily the best place to spend a Friday evening. If you wanted some quiet Sabbath time, you had to escape—maybe go out back or on the porch. I was thinking about calling some of my friends to see if maybe we could get together and go driving around. Not doing anything really bad, but certainly not doing what we should be doing on a Friday night. But then I thought about what Pastor Strickland had said. I went over to our little bookcase and said, "Mother, do we have the book *Christ Our Righteousness?*"

"No," she answered. "I've never heard of that book. We don't have it." Our little library was very, very small—some Spirit of Prophecy books, the missionary book of the year, a few others. Mom knew all the titles in the bookcase because she had read them many times. She said, "We don't have that book."

But for some reason, I kept looking. And down on the bottom shelf, there was a small book wrapped in brown paper. The title was stamped across the end of it, the way they used to do back then. And before I even saw what was written there, I just *knew* that book was going to be *Christ Our Righteousness*. I reached down and looked at it and read: *Christ Our Righteousness*! I tore the wrapping open and said, "Mom, when did you get this book?"

She said, "I've never seen it. I didn't get that." I think she must have gotten it at a book sale and just didn't realize it. But the Lord had been keeping it there for me to come across right at that particular time. I started reading it. I read that book through eight times before I touched another book. If you want to read a good book, read that one. It's powerful. Its whole message is wrapped up in this phrase: *The battle is the Lord's*. It's His battle. We don't win it; He does. He always has!

A while back, I heard about the "marshmallow" test. The people running the test took some three-year-old children and put them in a room. They placed two marshmallows in front of the kids and told them, "Don't eat these marshmallows. We're going to leave for a few minutes. If you don't eat the marshmallows, we'll give you even more marshmallows when we come back." Then they left for fifteen minutes and watched those kids through a one-way window.

Some kids had the marshmallows in their mouths before the door shut! Others kept reaching out and then pulling their hands back. Some of those poor little kids sat on their hands, trying to keep from putting a marshmallow in their mouth! The test was about delayed gratification. The researchers wanted to compare the kids who showed a lot of ability to delay gratification with those who didn't. Would more of the kids who delayed gratification finish school compared to the kids who ate the marshmallows right away? Would they do better in life?

By the way, if I had been one of those children they tested, I'd have messed up their study. I have never liked marshmallows! Sometimes they are OK if they're roasted just right, but I never can get them roasted right. They either burn or drop off in the fire! Now, if they had used Snickers bars for the test, I would have failed for sure! But you know what I thought of when I heard about that test? I thought, *I'm so thankful there is no marshmallow test when it comes to salvation.* Salvation is not about self-control. Salvation is all about the Lord. We talk about righteousness by faith, but there is no other kind of righteousness, is there? We have no righteousness of our own. Our good works don't earn us salvation.

I used to tease my good friend Don Schneider. He was German, as you can tell from his name. I'd say, "You know, Don, if salvation is by works, then only the Germans are going to be saved. They are the only ones with the discipline and the self-control to be saved!" But thank the Lord, it's not salvation by discipline. It's not salvation by self-control and good works. Salvation is all about the Lord. The Bible says, "The LORD does not save with sword and spear; for the battle is the LORD's" (1 Samuel 17:47).

When I was a conference president, we had worship every morning in the office. We didn't want to try to find something different to read each morning. We did that for a while, but it was boring. So we said, "Let's just read the Bible." That's what we did. We read the Bible through several times over the years, just reading a little bit every morning. Sometimes when we were reading in the Old Testament, someone would say, "Wow! The Bible is so bloody!"

That's because the Bible tells it like it is. It's real. The devil has been trying to destroy God's people throughout all of the earth's history. He tried to destroy the little band of people through whom God was going to bring the Messiah. Sometimes the only way that God could protect Israel was to annihilate the enemy. It had to happen. We may not like it, but it happened, and the Bible talks about it. But remember this, *It was God who brought the victory.* The Israelites were never victorious in their own strength. Never. When they tried to win battles by themselves, they lost. And when we attempt to win the battle, we'll lose as well. The battle is the Lord's.

God told His people in the Old Testament:

> "When you go out to battle against your enemies, and see horses and chariots and people more numerous than you, do not be afraid of them; for the LORD your God is with you. . . . When you are on the verge of battle, . . . the priest shall approach and speak to the people. And he shall say to them, 'Hear, O Israel: Today you are on the verge of battle with your enemies. Do not let your heart faint, do not be afraid, and do not tremble or be terrified because of them; for the LORD your God is He who goes with you, to fight for you against your enemies, to save you.' " (Deuteronomy 20:1–4)

You see, salvation has never been by works. In the Old Testament, salvation wasn't by works; it was by faith in God alone. It was by faith in the atoning power of the Savior who was coming. That is how victory came. That's still how it comes! It's a spiritual battle that we are in, and we can depend on the Lord our God to deliver us.

In 1 Samuel 17, we find the story of David and Goliath. We're all familiar with it. David, the young shepherd boy, was sent to bring provisions to his brothers who were in the army. David didn't go there to get into the battle. But once there, he realized that God was being profaned, and no one was doing anything about it. Saul, the king, should have gone out against Goliath; he should have known that it's

God who gives the victory, that the victory doesn't depend on your own strength and power. But Saul had lost sight of that. He had forgotten Deuteronomy 20—if he ever knew it.

But David knew it. That shepherd boy knew that when he had gone out against a bear and a lion, it wasn't his own strength that had brought victory. He knew that God had given him the victory! And he knew that God would give him the victory when he went up against Goliath. The battle was the Lord's.

> The Philistine said to David, "Am I a dog, that you come to me with sticks?" And the Philistine cursed David by his gods. . . . "Come to me, and I will give your flesh to the birds of the air and the beasts of the field!"
>
> Then David said to the Philistine, "You come to me with a sword, with a spear, and with a javelin. But I come to you in the name of the LORD of hosts, the God of the armies of Israel, whom you have defied. This day the LORD will deliver you into my hand, and I will strike you and take your head from you." (1 Samuel 17:43–46)

David was telling Goliath exactly what would happen— not because he was going to do this in his own strength, but because he knew that the Lord was going to use him to do it. The Lord was going to do it; David was just going to be the human instrument that God used. David said, "This day the LORD will deliver you into my hand, . . . that all the earth may know that there is a God in Israel. Then all this assembly shall know that the LORD does not save with sword and spear; for the battle is the LORD's, and He will give you into our hands" (verses 46, 47).

And that's exactly what happened. It took place just the way that David prophetically said it would take place. David wasn't speaking out of arrogance or some excessive confidence in himself. If that had been the case, he would have fallen before Goliath in failure. No, David stood there in the confidence of the Lord, knowing that He would give him the battle, for the battle is the Lord's.

When you read the rest of that chapter—1 Samuel 17— it's really fantastic. The Bible says that David took Goliath's head and brought it to Jerusalem, but the giant's weapons David kept in his tent (verse 54). He must have picked the head up by the hair to carry it, don't you think? I'm just using my imagination, but that's how I would carry it if I were David. I have a feeling that after nature had taken its course and all that was left was the skull, David still kept it. And I can imagine that when things got difficult, David might pull out that skull and say to himself, "God has brought me through all of this, and He's going to bring me through the rest."

Don't you have some skulls you bring out sometimes? Don't you have a sword that you've got hidden away in a tent that you bring out every once in a while? They remind you that if God has brought you through these things, He can bring you through whatever you're facing now. The battle is the Lord's!

Here is another story from the Bible. The enemies of God—the Moabites, the Ammonites, and some others—had come up to make war against Jehoshaphat, king of Judah. Jehoshaphat knew that he was no match for these armies.

So he prayed to God. It's one of the most beautiful prayers in Scripture:

> "O Lᴏʀᴅ God of our fathers, are You not God in heaven, and do You not rule over all the kingdoms of the nations, and in Your hand is there not power and might, so that no one is able to withstand You? Are You not our God, who drove out the inhabitants of this land before Your people Israel, and gave it to the descendants of Abraham Your friend forever? And they dwell in it, and have built You a sanctuary in it for Your name, saying, 'If disaster comes upon us—sword, judgment, pestilence, or famine—we will stand before this temple and in Your presence (for Your name is in this temple), and cry out to You in our affliction, and You will hear and save.' And now, here are the people of Ammon, Moab, and Mount Seir—whom You would not let Israel invade when they came out of the land of Egypt, but they turned from them and did not destroy them—here they are, rewarding us by coming to throw us out of Your possession which You have given us to inherit. O our God, will You not judge them? For we have no power against this great multitude that is coming against us; nor do we know what to do, but our eyes are upon You." (2 Chronicles 20:6–12)

Sometime when you are facing a real difficulty, pray that prayer. Put your circumstances in that prayer where Jehoshaphat's situation was. Claim God's promises, just as

Jehoshaphat did. It's a powerful prayer. God answered it for Jehoshaphat, and I believe He still answers it today for His faithful people.

Then when Jehoshaphat finished praying, God's Spirit came upon a young prophet, and this young prophet stood up to speak (verse 14). Do you know what he said? He said, "Listen, all you of Judah, and you inhabitants of Jerusalem, and you, King Jehoshaphat! Thus says the LORD to you: 'Do not be afraid nor dismayed because of this great multitude, for the battle is not yours, but God's' " (verse 15). It was the same message David had given. The battle is the Lord's—not yours, not mine, but God's!

We run around sometimes as if the battle depends entirely on us, but it doesn't. It depends on God. We need to rely on Him and trust Him. The young prophet counseled, "Tomorrow go down against them. They will surely come up by the Ascent of Ziz, and you will find them at the end of the brook before the Wilderness of Jeruel" (verse 16). In other words, "Don't wait for them to attack! Go out and meet them in the strength of the Lord." When you have difficulty, don't sit back. Go forward and face it. Don't run from it; go toward the battle, confident that it is not your battle, but God's.

Then the prophet told them, " 'You will not need to fight in this battle. Position yourselves, stand still and see the salvation of the LORD, who is with you, O Judah and Jerusalem!' Do not fear or be dismayed; tomorrow go out against them, for the LORD is with you" (verse 17). God cannot operate in a climate of fear; He operates in faith, not fear. When difficulty comes, He will be there. He is going to supply the victory.

Notice, the prophet didn't say, "Tomorrow, the Lord is going to take care of everything. Just sleep in, stay in your tent, and relax. The battle is the Lord's, so you don't have to do anything." No. He didn't say that. He said, "Go! Gird up and get ready!" The battle is the Lord's, but we don't know how much of it He is going to allow us to have a part in. We may not always know our role, but we do know what the outcome is going to be. If we go, we can trust Him to give us the victory.

Jehoshaphat and the people listened to the prophet, and they bowed down and worshiped God. Early the next morning, they went out to the battle. They didn't wait for the battle to come to them. As they set out, Jehoshaphat said, "Hear me, O Judah and you inhabitants of Jerusalem: Believe in the LORD your God, and you shall be established; believe His prophets, and you shall prosper" (verse 20).

They went out to the battle, singing praises to God! Sometimes preachers have put them in choir robes. I think they went out in battle gear, singing praise to the Lord as they marched. They were singing, "Praise the LORD, for His mercy endures forever" (verse 21). And as they were singing, the Lord "set ambushes" against their enemies. Their enemies turned on each other; they destroyed each other. The people of God never had to lift a finger because God fought the battle. The battle is the Lord's. With God, there is no defeat.

We must trust God for our salvation today. We must trust Him for our victory. He doesn't want us to be defeated continually. He defended Israel because He didn't want to see them go down in defeat. He wanted them to have victory.

David was victorious over the giant because He went to

the battle trusting the Lord's strength. Later in life, Bathsheba showed up, and temptation was able to do what the giant couldn't. Temptation defeated David because he tried to fight the battle in his own strength. When David saw Bathsheba, if he had begun to sing some of those beautiful psalms he had written, if he had begun to praise the Lord and ask the Lord for victory in the battle that was taking place in his heart—I think the Lord would have answered his prayer and lust would have gone away. David would have seen that temptation for what it was—a hideous sin—instead of being drawn to it and then eventually committing murder to try to cover it up. David would have been victorious in that battle.

But you know the great thing about our God is that even when we take things into our own hands and foul up completely, He still has a plan for victory. God's plan was to pick David back up and cleanse him from his sin. David paid a price for his sin; he didn't get away with it. Don't think that he did. He virtually lost his family; the whole rebellion problem with his son Absalom was caused by that sin. He paid a price, but God forgave him.

Like David, you may have lost a battle with temptation. But God can still give you victory. The battle is still the Lord's. David was a great sinner, but he was also a great repenter. He confessed his sin and asked the Lord for forgiveness. That can be your experience as well.

The battle is the Lord's!

Chapter Four

LIVING
WATER

છ

Jesus answered and said to her . . . "Whoever
drinks of the water that I shall give him will
never thirst. But the water that I shall give
him will become in him a fountain of water
springing up into everlasting life."
—John 4:13, 14

I love John's Gospel. It's my favorite book of all of my favorite
books of the Bible. For me, John's Gospel contains familiar
texts that I've loved and known and memorized for most of
my life. Texts such as John 3:16, probably the best-known text
in the Bible: "For God so loved the world that He gave His only
begotten Son, that whoever believes in Him should not perish
but have everlasting life." Or another favorite of mine: "Let not
your heart be troubled; you believe in God, believe also in Me.
. . . I go to prepare a place for you. And if I go and prepare a
place for you, I will come again and receive you to Myself; that
where I am, there you may be also" (John 14:1–3).

And it's in John's Gospel that we find the story of Jesus meeting a woman at a well in Samaria. It's a familiar story— one we've heard many times. But I believe that in these familiar stories, there are always new things that God would have us learn and understand, things that will grip our hearts. The story begins with Jesus deciding to leave Judea and go back up to Galilee. "But He needed to go through Samaria" (John 4:4).

Why did He "need" to go through Samaria on His way to Galilee? If you look at a map, at first glance, it looks like the most direct route from Judea and Jerusalem to Galilee goes through Samaria. But you should look again.

In Jesus' day, the best route was to go northeast to Jericho and then cross the Jordan River and go north to Galilee, following the river along its east bank and bypassing Samaria altogether. In the first place, the road through Samaria was terrible. It was in Jesus' day, and it still is. It's a very winding road because it follows the natural terrain. When we put in a road or freeway today, we pretty much cut straight through the mountains. Back then, they wound around through the mountains, following the easiest path. This meant a lot of winding switchbacks, so that road through Samaria was actually longer than the more roundabout way that bypassed Samaria.

But there was another reason not to go through Samaria. At that time, Jews had absolutely nothing to do with Samaritans. If fact, even if the easiest route from Judea to Galilee had been through Samaria, the Jews still wouldn't have gone that way. Samaritans and Jews were enemies. Devout Jews went out of their way to avoid having anything to do with Samaritans.

It had not always been that way. In fact, back in Solomon's time, Judea and the area that would come to be known as Samaria had all been part of the same kingdom. During his reign, Solomon had been intent on building up a tremendous dynasty, on building the temple, on making Jerusalem so magnificent that people came from around the then-known world to look at that city because of its beauty and its riches. But all this had cost a lot of money. Solomon had taxed Israel heavily. The people in the north part of the country felt especially taxed and put upon. Everyone was required to give a certain amount of time and labor in constructing the temple and city, which meant that the people in the north had to leave their homes and come to the south to work in Jerusalem as well as to pay heavy taxes.

When Solomon died, his son Rehoboam came to the throne. The people came to him and said, "Are you going to be hard on us like your father was, or are you going to let up?"

Rehoboam went to his advisors before answering. The old men told him, "Tell the people that you're going to ease up on them, that you're not going to be as exacting as your father has been."

But the young men said, "Oh no, that's a sign of weakness. Don't do that! Tell the people that they haven't seen anything yet! Tell them you are going to be harder on them than your father was."

Rehoboam took the wrong counsel. He followed the advice of the young men. The result was that the kingdom split. Jeroboam, a natural-born leader in the north, peeled off the ten northern tribes, leaving Rehoboam with Judah and Benjamin in the south.

Still, the northern and southern parts of the kingdom remained allies to the extent that if some other nation jumped on them, they would band together against the common enemy. But internally, they were separate. Everyone, north and south, still worshiped God at the temple in Jerusalem—until about 720 B.C. when Assyria attacked the north and defeated it completely. Assyria decided that the best way to truly rule the northern kingdom was to bring in people from other nations and settle them there in Israel. They went even further, trying to mingle nationalities. They decreed that Jewish young men and Jewish young women must marry one of these foreigners who had been settled in their land. Jews couldn't marry Jews. As a result, Jews in the south began to look upon the people in the north as a mixed-race—not really Jews.

Now the split became more pronounced than ever. Eventually, north and south hardly even spoke the same language! Then the people in the south were taken into Babylonian captivity. When they came back and started to rebuild Jerusalem, the northerners said, "We'll help you." But the southerners responded, "We don't need your help." And the split widened even more.

Then the Samaritans, the northerners, built a temple on Mount Gerazim and said, "We don't have to go to Jerusalem anymore to worship. We have our own temple up here." And their worship began to take a different direction. It contained elements of the truth about God, but it included a lot of other things as well. The division was now so complete that a devout Jew would not even allow a Samaritan's shadow to fall on him for fear of being defiled! That's how intense the feeling was. Can you imagine what the Samaritans thought about that?

By Jesus' time, Jews would avoid Samaria at all costs. So why would Jesus choose to go through Samaria rather than taking the easier route? Why does the Bible say Jesus "needed to go through Samaria"?

He needed to go through Samaria because there was a lost woman there who needed Him. Just one woman. A Samaritan woman.

Scientists used to tell us there were 65,000 galaxies. Then they increased the number to 100,000 galaxies and then increased it further to 250,000 galaxies. Then the Hubble telescope came along, and now they tell us that there are innumerable galaxies in the universe. They can't calculate the number of galaxies that are out there. Let's say that in each galaxy there is only one inhabited planet—just one! I think it's terribly exclusive for us to think that we're the only place in the entire universe that's inhabited. But let's say that just one planet in each galaxy is inhabited. Here we are in the one inhabited planet in our galaxy, and there is one woman on our planet in one small town in a despised place who needs Jesus. And He's going to find her! That's the kind of God that we worship. He's not a distant God who remains somewhere far off. He's a personal God. He knows you. The Bible says He knows the number of the hairs on your head (Matthew 10:30). Some people present more of a challenge in that regard than others, but it still remains a remarkable fact! The Bible says God knows when a sparrow falls (verse 29). Oh, what a God! And we see this personalized love demonstrated in the way that Jesus sought this woman.

Now, this woman was not good. She wasn't the most honest woman in town. She was not the most virtuous

person in town. Jesus didn't go to her because of her goodness; He went to her because of her need. You know, sometimes, we tend to count people's worth by their goodness,
but God's love for us doesn't depend on how worthy we
are. He loves us all equally—good, bad, or indifferent.
And Jesus loved that Samaritan woman. She was a sinner,
but that didn't affect His love for her. John tells us: "He
[Jesus] came to a city of Samaria which is called Sychar,
near the plot of ground that Jacob gave to his son Joseph.
Now Jacob's well was there. Jesus therefore, being wearied
from His journey, sat thus by the well. It was about the
sixth hour" (John 4:5, 6).

The "sixth hour," according to Jewish reckoning, would
be what we know as noon. But in the Roman way of keeping
time, the "sixth hour" is what we would call six o'clock in
the afternoon. Now, it isn't really important whether it was
noon or six o'clock when Jesus sat down at the well. The fact
of the matter is that when the New Testament talks about
time, it is usually referring to Roman time because the Jews
were under Roman rule in the days of Jesus. But that isn't
always the case.

I've heard preachers telling this story who say that the
woman came to the well at noon because she knew it would
be less likely that anyone else would be there at that time—
that she didn't want to have to meet anyone and have them
gossiping about her. It's OK to have some sanctified imagination, but I don't much agree with that idea. Because the
more I find out about this woman as the story unfolds,
the more I'm convinced that she had quit worrying about
gossip a long time before Jesus showed up. Somewhere along
the line—maybe around husband number three or four or

five—she had gotten to the place where she really didn't care what anyone said about her. If anyone had something to say about her, she probably came right back with something to say about them or their husband or their family. Just look at the way she comes back at Jesus in her conversation with Him! This woman stands up to Jesus when He talks with her!

Six o'clock in the afternoon makes a little more sense, too, when you consider that it was about a day's walk from the area of Jerusalem up to Sychar in Samaria. So arriving tired at six o'clock seems to fit the facts. Of course, back then, there wasn't a Wendy's or a McDonald's along the road, so travelers had to plan their eating. They generally planned on eating their main meal in the evening. The next morning, for breakfast, they would eat a little of what was leftover from the night before. Then they would carry a small portion of food with them and eat it sometime during the middle of the day as they walked. That night, they would find a place to stop and buy more food. The Bible says the disciples had gone into Sychar to buy food (John 4:8). To me, all this seems to point to six o'clock in the afternoon as the time Jesus met the woman at the well.

Jesus was tired after walking all day (verse 6). The Creator, the great God who created this world—tired? That's kind of hard for us to wrap our minds around. This whole idea of Jesus becoming a human like us—that's not easy to understand.

A woman asked me one time, "What do you believe about the nature of Christ—His divinity and His humanity?" You know, that's a big issue with some people.

I said, "I believe Jesus was one hundred percent human

and one hundred percent divine." Now, I can't explain that, but I believe it.

She kept on. "Did Jesus have the nature of Adam before the Fall or after the Fall?"

"Let me ask you a question," I answered. "What nature did Adam have before the Fall?"

"Oh," she said, "he had a perfect nature."

"That's right," I told her, "And what good did that perfect nature seem to be for Adam? He went down just like that when tempted, didn't he? With a perfect nature, he fell for the first temptation that came along."

You see, I'm not going to worry too much about what kind of human nature Jesus had. I know this: His life was perfect, and His perfect life stands in the place of my imperfect life. And I pray that He will give me strength and victory when temptation comes. It all comes from Him.

There are a lot of things I don't understand. I don't even try to understand some things. Instead, I want to understand *Jesus*! I want to know about *Him.* Focus upon *Him.* Let me tell you, don't focus on the doubts and the questions; focus on the Answer!

Sometimes people ask me, "How can you believe in Creation?" Let me tell you. It's very, very simple. I don't base my belief in Creation on what Moses says—although I believe I could base it on Moses. I base my belief in Creation on Jesus. The Bible says that Jesus is the Creator (Colossians 1:16; John 1:1–3), so I believe it and accept it. Somebody says, "Well, we've been studying the rocks, and the rocks tell us . . ." You go ahead and study the rocks. But I'm going to study the Rock of Ages. And He tells me that He is the Creator. You never go wrong believing what Jesus says.

And there Jesus was, sitting on the edge of the well, resting because He was tired from walking all day. Then the woman showed up with her water jug. "Jesus said to her, 'Give Me a drink' " (John 4:7).

The woman was surprised and startled. She immediately recognized something remarkable was taking place. First of all, men didn't speak to women—period. I don't know how men and women became acquainted back then because they didn't talk to each other. Especially, religious leaders didn't speak with women. In fact, there was a group of Pharisees who were called "the bruised and bleeding Pharisees" because they wore blinders to avoid even looking at a woman. With these blinders on, they could look only down at their feet, so they were frequently walking into a wall or a tree or something and bruising themselves or cutting themselves. That's why they were called "the bruised and bleeding Pharisees."

The Samaritan woman could tell from Jesus' garments that He was a rabbi. Here was a religious Jew talking to a woman! She couldn't believe her ears. "How is it that You, being a Jew, ask a drink from me, a Samaritan woman?"(verse 9).

And Jesus replied, "If you knew . . . who it is who says to you, 'Give Me a drink,' you would have asked Him, and He would have given you living water" (verse 10).

Now, when we hear the words "living water," we immediately think of something spiritual—the water of life that slakes our spiritual thirst. But "living water" can also mean simply "running water"—running water as in a stream or river as opposed to water in a well. The woman wasn't sure if Jesus was talking about something spiritual or something physical, but she knew that she wanted it—whatever it was.

"Sir," she said, "give me this water" (verse 15).

And Jesus replied, " 'Go, call your husband, and come here.' The woman answered and said, 'I have no husband.' Jesus said to her, 'You have well said, "I have no husband," for you have had five husbands, and the one whom you now have is not your husband' " (verses 17, 18).

Clearly, this woman was not good at what we call interpersonal relationships. In fact, she was a complete, total failure in that department. She had had five husbands and hadn't bothered to marry the man she was living with currently.

Was Jesus being mean to her when He asked her to go get her husband? No. He was letting her know that He knew everything about her. He knew the worst about her, and yet He still cared for her. You see, Jesus meets you and me at the well of life, and He makes us feel comfortable with Him. That's the difference between Jesus and some "righteous" people. Some "righteous" people meet you, and you figure out right away that there is no way you can ever be as "righteous" as they are. You tell them you're a vegetarian, and they say, "I'm a vegan!" You tell them you're a vegan, and they say, "I eat only raw vegetables!" It just goes on and on. You cannot be more righteous than they are! But Jesus meets you and me where we are; He's not going to leave us there, but He makes us feel comfortable as He takes us to a better place. He's going to lead us and guide us—not drive us. He loves us like He loved this Samaritan woman, and He will meet us at the well just as He arranged to meet her.

Jesus is still saving the lost. We like to find people to save that are pretty clean already. We look at someone, and we say to ourselves, "All right, this person doesn't smoke, doesn't drink, and is careful about what he eats. He'll make a perfect

Adventist! All I have to do is convince him about the state of the dead and switch him over to worship on the Sabbath—and he's ready to go!" That's it! Minor adjustments.

But what about your neighbor in his backyard? You know, the guy who has the burnt offering going out there on his grill, with the can of beer in his hand, and a cigar in his mouth. His wife won't let him smoke in the house, but you can smell it all the way over at your house, it's so bad. Do you go out there in the backyard and visit with him? Talk with him? If you did, you might find the most fantastic person you've ever run into—he just needs Jesus. And when he finds Jesus, what a difference that will make in his life.

I remember a young couple down in Louisiana. The Adventist pastor was studying with them. These people were into everything you could think of in a lifestyle out of harmony with Jesus. One night, my pastor friend began to study the Bible with them. The Bible study lasted all night, and by morning they didn't smoke anymore; they didn't drink anymore; there were a lot of things they didn't do anymore. Now, this was not the pastor's doing; it was the Holy Spirit's doing. It was the Lord's doing. The Lord cleaned them up in one night! When I talked to them later, they said, "Don't tell us that God can't save you and change your life in a single night. He did that for us. We couldn't get enough; we just drank it in." Jesus was pouring out the living water, and they were drinking it and drinking it and drinking it! What a change! When I talk to those people today, I can't believe they ever lived the way that they told me they used to live. God has cleaned them up so thoroughly that it's hard to imagine that those things used to be a part of their lives. He changed them, just like He changed the woman at the well.

Jesus offered her living water that would quench her thirst completely. He changed her life. And the record is that she went back into Sychar and told her neighbors and friends and everyone what had happened (John 4:39–42). She said to them, "I want you to come and meet a man who told me everything that I've ever done. Some of you know some of the things I've done, but He knows *everything*, and He still loves me! He has forgiven me and cleansed me. This is the Messiah!"

The people listened to her, and they came. "Many of the Samaritans of that city believed in Him because of the word of the woman. . . . And many more believed because of His own word" (verses 39, 41).

When the disciples got back from buying food in the city, they said, "Lord, we're pretty hungry; it's time to eat."

And He said, "I have food to eat of which you do not know" (verse 32).

"Has anyone brought Him anything to eat?" they asked each other (verse 33).

They were missing the whole point. Jesus was no longer tired and hungry because when you share life with someone, it brings life to you. When you share what Jesus has given you, you don't lose a thing; you only gain more as you do it.

God is still saving people and cleaning them up. When I went over to the city of Kharkiv in Ukraine to hold evangelistic meetings, we had a fantastic time and baptized about fifteen hundred people. A few years later, I went back to the same place. A lot of things had changed in the meantime. The church had grown, and that was good. But prices for everything had gone up unbelievably, and that wasn't so good. Before, I had stayed in a hotel and had a pretty good room as far as rooms there go. It cost eleven dollars a day. When I returned, that same room was now one hundred dollars a day!

I said, "Can't you give me a little better price?" And they wouldn't. They had found out about the European and American markets and had even gone beyond it. At eleven dollars a day, that was a good room, but it didn't have the quality to be a one-hundred-dollar-a-day room. I told the pastor, "Look, I'm going to be here for a month. Thirty days at one hundred dollars a day would be three thousand dollars! With that much money, I could help start a church. I could help build a church. I don't want to give three thousand dollars for a hotel room. Do you have a place I can sleep?"

He said, "Would you come to my house and sleep?"

"Sure," I replied. "Sure, I would."

He said, "I have a couch."

I said, "All right. You don't mind?"

"No," he said, "I don't mind. Do you mind?"

"No," I told him, "I don't mind."

Now I'm going to tell you something. Neither that couch nor my back will ever be the same. When I left there, I had to leave him some money for a new couch. But there was nothing he could do about my back! But the Lord blessed.

Before, we had brought a team with us. This time, we didn't have the money to bring a team. When we first started going over to the USSR, our people were so generous that we had money to go over there and do some things. But now it was harder to raise money, so the only person I could bring with me was a translator. That's all. When we got there, I asked the people, "Who is going to take care of the music?"

"Oh, we have somebody to do the music," they assured me. "We have Tonya."

I said, "Tonya?"

They said, "Don't you remember Tonya?"

I said, "No, I don't."

They said, "We baptized Tonya when you were here before." It had been five years since I had been there the first time.

"Tell me about Tonya," I said.

They said, "Tonya was a nightclub singer, and one night she was walking through the park where we were holding the meetings in a large theater. She heard music coming out of the theater, and she was drawn in by the music. Then she stayed for the message. She never missed a night after that and was baptized at the end of the meetings. Don't you remember her?"

I said, "There were some fifteen hundred people baptized. I must be honest. I don't remember Tonya."

Well, when I was ready to come out and preach that first night, Tonya was singing. I still didn't remember her. But you see, God had done some remarkable things in that woman's life. She had been a nightclub singer. Her marriage was practically no marriage at all—just mostly something on paper. But her husband, Uri, began to see a change in her. He told her, "Something's happened to you. Tell me about it." So she told him about Jesus and about coming to the meetings. Uri said, "I want to go to church with you." The meetings had ended by this time, but Uri started going to church with her.

Tonya's mother was an old, hard, cold communist, but she saw the change in Tonya and in Uri. She told them, "I want to go to church with you." Their daughter was a teenager, already mature beyond her years, and living a lifestyle that was totally out of harmony with God's will. She, too, saw the change in her mother and father; she saw the love that had come into the home. She saw that there were meals on the table now where there hadn't been much of that before. She saw some dramatic changes in her parents' lives. And she said, "I want to go to church with you." And she did.

Tonya quit singing in the nightclub and started to work in a beauty salon. Another stylist at the salon had known Tonya for a long time, and she saw how different Tonya's life had become. She said, "My husband and I want to go to church with you."

That night when Tonya was singing before I began to preach, the sound man sitting out in the audience was her husband, Uri. On one side of Uri was his mother-in-law; on the other side was his daughter, who was organizing the background tapes that her mother sang with and handing them to her father at the right time. To her left was the couple who had been baptized as a result of working with Tonya at the salon. Next to them were another friend and his wife, whom Tonya had brought to the meetings and would be baptized before the meetings ended.

That is what happens when God changes a life! It's fantastic. It's tremendous. He can take lives that we think have absolutely no possibility of being changed, and He can do something with those lives. I can't do it; you can't do it. We can't change these people, but the Spirit of God can—and will.

In the city of Dnipropetrovsk, during some meetings I held, there was a man who came night after night. I don't know if you can quite visualize this or not, but some people have drank and smoked so much that even their skin color seems to be affected by it. I mean that. It's almost like they've been put in a smokehouse and been smoked for a while. This man looked like that. He had tattoos all over his arms. He came to the meetings night after night. I could see him out there in the audience.

Now, it was very dim outside the little hotel where we were staying, and it was in a very rough neighborhood. In that part of the world, the only people who stay in hotels are mafia members and American evangelists! We were the latter. One night, we went back to the hotel after the meeting had ended. As we got out of the car, several local Adventist ministers were with us; they had me covered. Let me tell you. Those fellows are something. Those preachers over there have all been in the military. They were surrounding me to keep me safe because they were afraid. And all of a sudden, this tattooed man from the meetings came right through that ring of Adventist ministers! They tried to grab him. "No! No, he's OK," I said, because I'd seen him every night at the meetings.

"I have given my life to Satan," he said and raised up his shirt. There was a satanic tattoo right over his heart. "But now," he continued, "I want to give my life to Jesus."

And I said, "Let's pray." I put my hand on his tattoo and prayed, "God, release this man from satanic influences and fill him with the power of Your Holy Spirit. Sustain him. Save him. Father, this alcohol that's on his breath—take it away from him. Take the tobacco away from him, take the drugs. Whatever he has in his life that shouldn't be there, Father, take it away from him and give him Your life. Give him the living water."

When he left, I'll confess that I thought, *There's no way he's going to make it. Lord, it can happen only through You. You're the only way, the only way.* A few nights later, I gave a call, and the first person to get to his feet was this man. He didn't *walk* down the aisle; he came *running*! Someone had a video camera going, and we caught a picture of that man running down the aisle to give his life to Jesus.

Six months later, I went back to that city and wondered, *Is he still there?* He was still there. I returned other times, and sometimes I'd see him. If he wasn't there, I'd ask about him. People would say, "He's out to sea. He's a sailor, but he's true. He loves the Lord. He's given his life to Him. He's changed."

The last time I saw him, we were in an auditorium with people standing packed everywhere. Every square inch was occupied by a body. I looked up in the balcony, and there he was. I was preaching with a translator, and when you're preaching with a translator, you preach awhile, and then while the translator is telling them what you said, you can get ready for what you are going to say next. So while my translator was speaking, I stepped over to where I could see this man and pointed at him, and I smiled the biggest smile I could smile. And he motioned back with both hands. I knew what he meant. He was telling me, *God is still working in me to live for Him.* Jesus still saves today like He saved the woman at the well!

If you've never tasted the living water Jesus offers, would you like to do so right now? You can accept Him right now.

He can clean you up. He can do it; I know He can. If you will accept Him right where you are, He will accept you right where you are as well. Won't you do that now? Say, "Yes, Jesus, come into my life. Fill me with living water."

Chapter Five

THE
JOY OF
JESUS

ch

"These things I have spoken to you,
that My joy may remain in you,
and that your joy may be full."
—*John 15:11*

With all the channels you can get on cable TV, it seems there is a channel for everything. Have you ever watched the weather channel? Don't do that. I tell people, "Don't watch the weather channel; it will scare you to death!" I've known people who watch the weather channel all day, and they get afraid to leave their house when they see all the predictions of storms and tornados and floods.

You see, the only thing the weather channel has to talk about is the weather, so they make it as dramatic as they can. I saw a reporter on the weather channel the other day talking about a 20 percent chance of rain. You'd think a disaster was about to happen. A 20 percent chance of rain? Why not talk about an 80 percent chance of sunshine? I guess that wouldn't make the news. Why do we have this tendency to look at everything from a negative point of view?

The Bible lists the fruits of the Holy Spirit: "The fruit of the Spirit is love, joy, peace, longsuffering, kindness, goodness, faithfulness, gentleness, self-control. Against such there is no law" (Galatians 5:22, 23).

I believe with all of my heart that we belong to a group of Christians who are a loving group of people. Everywhere I go, I find a lot of love. We have patience—for the most part. I see a lot of kindness in our people. But there is one fruit of the Spirit that I don't see as often as I should—joy. It's the second in the list, but it seems to come way down toward the end of our Christian experience. Some of us seem to have the idea that joy just isn't something Christians should have too much of. But the Bible says joy is one of the fruits of the Spirit; in fact, it is second on the list.

Where did we ever get the idea that we were not to have joy? Where did we ever come up with the idea that Christians should go around long-faced and solemn? The Bible doesn't teach that. In fact, look up the word *joy* sometime in a Bible concordance. You'll find a lot of references where joy is mentioned in the Bible. Here are a few:

- Deuteronomy 28:47: "Serve the Lord your God with joy and gladness of heart."
- Nehemiah 8:10: "For the joy of the Lord is your strength."
- Nehemiah 12:43: "God had made them rejoice with great joy."
- Job 38:7: "All the sons of God shouted for joy."

- Psalm 5:11: "Let those also who love Your name be joyful in You."
- Psalm 32:11: "Shout for joy, all you upright in heart!"
- Isaiah 51:11: "The ransomed of the LORD shall return, and come to Zion with singing, with everlasting joy on their heads."
- John 15:11: "These things I have spoken to you, that My joy may remain in you, and that your joy may be full."
- Acts 13:52: "The disciples were filled with joy and with the Holy Spirit."
- 1 Peter 1:8: "Rejoice with joy inexpressible and full of glory."

The list goes on and on throughout the Scriptures. God wants us to have joy. We need joy because we face a lot of challenges, don't we? It's not easy to live in the world right now. It has never been easy to live in this world of sin, and we need something to sustain us. The fruits of the Spirit are designed to do just that. They are to be a part of us. We need that love to sustain us; we need peace to sustain us; we need joy to sustain us.

Now, the joy that the Bible talks about is different from happiness. Happiness is sort of related to circumstances and happenstance. If the circumstances are just right, then you're happy. But that's not joy. When you have joy, it's there whatever the circumstances. It has nothing to do with happenstance. Joy is an undergirding emotion, an undergirding principle of life that you have regardless of the circumstances around you.

Sometimes people say, *If only . . .* If only I had more money, then I would have joy! You know, that has been proven not to be true over and over. Studies have been done on people who have won the lottery. Almost without exception, ten years after winning the lottery, the winners say that if they could go back in time, they would choose not to have won. Money didn't bring them joy.

Now, I know some of you reading that are saying to yourself, *I don't know about that. I'd rather be miserable and rich than miserable and poor!* But, believe me, money doesn't bring joy. Often, it doesn't even bring a lot of happiness.

Some people think, *If I were just better looking, that would bring joy. If I were just thinner . . . ,* or *If I were just heavier . . .* When I was young, I played sports in school. Believe it or not, in those days, I was so thin that my coaches would try to get me to gain weight. One coach told me, "If I could just put twenty pounds on you, it would give your fastball so much more zip!" So he put me on six meals a day, and he gave me some kind of odd weight-gain stuff that I was to drink. But I didn't gain any weight. (I want to warn you about that odd weight-gain drink. It doesn't work immediately, but it kicks in about ten years later!) Women, especially, think, *If I were just thinner . . .* But let me tell you something. We need to have joy right now, right where we are today, whether we're thin or heavy, short or tall!

What about talent? Does having a lot of talent bring joy? Not necessarily. God can use you with whatever amount of talent you have. That's what brings joy—letting God use you to carry out His purposes. Some of those who have the most talent refuse to let God really use that talent. They don't have joy just because they are talented more than others.

The joy that comes from Jesus is something that happens in an experience with Him that has absolutely nothing to do with the circumstances around us. Of course, there are some things we like a lot more than we like other things. It's certainly more fun to attend a joyful wedding than a sad funeral. But the joy of Jesus sees us through every challenge that comes to us as we live in Jesus Christ.

I want to introduce you to a man in Scripture—a man who didn't even become a Christian until he was grown. This man was on his way to persecute a few Christians when suddenly he had an encounter with Jesus Christ. Jesus called him in a very dramatic way to serve Him as an apostle. He was to do a great work for God. Now, you would think that a man called like this, a man with such potential and value in God's work would have a bubble of protection built around him. You'd think that God would protect him completely from every harm and danger.

Look at what the apostle Paul wrote about that: "In prisons more frequently, in deaths often. From the Jews five times I received forty stripes minus one. Three times I was beaten with rods; once I was stoned; three times I was shipwrecked . . . in journeys often, in perils of waters, in perils of robbers . . . in perils in the city, in perils in the wilderness, in perils in the sea" (2 Corinthians 11:23–26).

He says, "Five times I received forty stripes minus one." We tend to read that and move right on. But stop and think about that for a minute. This was a beating that came within an inch of taking a person's life. The whip was made of long leather lashes, and at the end of each of those lashes was a sharp piece of metal or stone. The person had to bare his back and lean over something. When the whip came down full force on his bare back, the person doing the beating would jerk those leather lashes across the body, and the sharp metal at the ends would tear the flesh right off. At the end of thirty-nine strokes, your back looked like roadkill.

Paul says he suffered this kind of beating *five times*! Can you imagine? The first time, the second time, the third time, the fourth time, the fifth time—Paul must have been thinking, *Lord, why? Why?* And yet, he kept preaching the gospel.

"Once I was stoned," he writes (verse 25). One stoning was usually enough! Stoning kept on until the person being stoned was dead. They thought Paul was dead (Acts 14:19). It wasn't a halfway stoning job. They intended to kill him, and they thought they had. What happened? Paul was lying there unconscious. Then, he began to move a little, and his friends who had come to get his body started to remove the stones. They saw he wasn't quite dead, so they nursed him back to life. And he lived! When he had recovered, did he say, "Well, that's it. I've given it everything I have, and I just don't have anything more to give"? No, Paul kept going and giving.

"Three times I was shipwrecked." Three times! I'm sure Paul prayed for a safe journey before he got on a ship. When our family gets in a car and goes on a trip, we have a prayer. We get on a plane—we have prayer. The other day I missed a plane, and I want to tell you that I was not happy about it! I was at the airport, actually at the gate. I stepped away from the gate just for a few minutes, and during that time, they loaded the plane and closed the flight!

When I came back, they said, "We're sorry!"

I said, "The plane hasn't left yet."

They said, "We're sorry. We have closed the flight."

I said, "You closed the flight twenty minutes early; it's not supposed to be closed yet."

They said, "We're sorry. But we have closed the flight."

I was upset. Then I thought about Paul. Would missing a flight have upset Paul? It's so easy for us to read about Paul's trials and sufferings and just move on. Shipwrecked three times! In perils in the sea. Put yourself on that ship and think about what was happening to Paul. He says, "A night and a day I have been in the deep" (2 Corinthians 11:25). How would you like to spend a night and day floating on the ocean, hanging on to a piece of wrecked ship? A whole night and a day!

He says, "In perils among false brethren" (verse 26). Elder H. M. S. Richards told me one time, "Sometimes I've had conflict with the brethren. At the time, I thought they were false brethren. Then, as I have matured, I realized that they were sincere brethren just like I was a sincere brother, but we just had different opinions."

Paul didn't just have problems with a brother who was difficult to get along with. He was in perils with some really, truly false brethren. He says, "In weariness and toil, in sleeplessness often, in hunger and thirst, in fasting often, in cold and nakedness—besides the other things, what comes upon me daily: my deep concern for all the churches" (verses 27, 28).

Stress! Suffering! Danger! Paul had it all. But through it all, he never quit. When he was finally arrested and taken to Rome and put into prison, he was chained to guards. Did he get upset? No. He witnessed to the guards. He must have thought, *I have a captive audience, someone I can talk to about Jesus.* His guards took the message of the gospel back to the palace; that is how the gospel grew so rapidly among the elite in Rome. While he was in prison and couldn't do much else, Paul wrote the prison epistles that we have in the Bible. They have been a tremendous blessing down through the centuries.

One of those epistles he wrote from prison in Rome was his letter to the Philippians. In that letter, in its four short chapters, Paul uses the word *joy* or a synonym for joy nineteen times.

"I thank my God," he wrote, "upon every remembrance of you, always in every prayer of mine making request for you with all joy" (Philippians 1:3, 4).

In chapter 2, "Therefore if there is any consolation in Christ, if any comfort of love, if any fellowship of the Spirit, if any affection and mercy, fulfill my joy by being like-minded, having the same love" (verses 1, 2).

Then in Philippians 4:4, he says, "Rejoice in the Lord always. Again I will say, rejoice!" That's what God wants us to do—rejoice in the Lord always!

Finally, he voices one of the secrets, one of the great principles of his joy. "I have learned in whatever state I am, to be content: I can do all things through Christ who strengthens me" (verses 11, 13). Paul could handle whatever came his way because his joy was centered in Jesus Christ. We need to learn that principle of joy in Christ. We need to have a joy transfusion!

Some things will steal our joy. If we dwell on the past, that can steal our joy. Worrying about mistakes from our past can steal our joy. As a pastor, I've spent a lot of time visiting with people about spiritual things. Often they have regrets. There are things they have done that they wished they had not done. Things they have said that they wished they had not said. The past can steal our joy if we dwell on those things and worry about the things we wish had been different.

The future, too, can steal our joy. Worrying about the future will steal our joy. Being concerned about the future of our families or for the things that are to come upon the world can steal our joy. Some Christians are so concerned about the coming time of trouble that they can't have any joy in their lives right now. We need to let the time of trouble come when it's ready to come, when God is ready for it to come and instead focus on living a life of joy in Christ right now day by day.

It's the same with the problems facing the world today—financial problems, climate problems, political problems, crime, and disasters. We don't have to ignore these things and put our heads in the sand. We should do what we can to help and be responsible citizens of the world. But God hasn't put you and me on the committee to predict the time of His return and lose our joy by worrying ourselves unduly about world conditions.

Thirty-five years ago, a lady came to me and said, "Pastor, I don't know if I'm going to be able to make it through the time of trouble." She was so concerned about that. I saw her not long ago—and she's still concerned about making it through the time of trouble! Thirty-five years of missing out on the joys of today because of a concern about the future! Jesus says, "These things I have spoken to you, that My joy may remain in you, and that your joy may be full" (John 15:11). "I want you to have My joy," He says. We need to live in the joy of the moment because that is what Jesus wants us to do. We can't go back and relive the past.

And we can't go forward and live in the future. Today, right now, is all we really have. And that time can be filled with the joy that Jesus gives.

Helen Mallicoat wrote a poem titled, "I Am."

> I was regretting the past
> And fearing the future.
> Suddenly my Lord was speaking:
>
> "My name is I AM." He paused.
> I waited. He continued,
> "When you live in the past
> With its mistakes and regrets,
> It is hard. I am not there,
> My name is not I WAS.
>
> "When you live in the future
> With its problems and fears,
> It is hard. I am not there.
> My name is not I WILL BE.
>
> "When you live in this moment,
> It is not hard. I am here.
> My name is I AM."

Jesus says, "I am the way, the truth, and the life" (John 14:6). If you would have Him as your Savior, if you would have Him as the power in your life right now, you have to rely upon Him totally and completely and allow Him to help you no matter what you're facing. No matter what difficulties you face today, hold on to Jesus! There are a lot of people today who live in pain, and they wonder, *How can I have joy when I live in such pain?* The only way to do that is to *choose* to have joy. Say, "I am going to trust in Jesus as my Savior, as my Sustainer, and I am not going to allow this arthritis (or whatever pain or suffering or problem you are facing) to rob me of the joy that I have in Jesus Christ my Lord." Sometimes, we don't realize how much our Lord cares about us in every aspect of our lives, and how much He wants us to have joy.

This idea may sound crazy. Can we really choose joy? But John 15:11 assures us that joy is a gift that Christ gives to us. Jesus says, "I want to give you My joy so that your joy may be complete." His joy makes our joy complete. We don't have any joy without His. What we have is not joy unless it's united with His joy. Then it's complete, and we can trust Him.

No matter how complicated our life is when we turn it over to Jesus and start trusting in Him, He sees us through every one of the challenges we face. He'll do it! Jesus wants you to face each challenge with His joy in you. You can do it. Right now, you can receive the joy of Jesus. He says, "These things I have spoken to you, that My joy may remain in you, and that your joy may be full" (verse 11).

Chapter Six

THANK
YOU

＆

Give thanks to the LORD, for He is good!
For His mercy endures forever.
—Psalm 106:1

In everything give thanks; for this is the will of
God in Christ Jesus for you.
—1 Thessalonians 5:18

The Seventh-day Adventist Church has meant everything to me. This church brought me Jesus Christ,
and I am thankful for that.

My mother was a Seventh-day Adventist, and my father
was a Presbyterian. He was a good man, a moral man, an
honest man—as honest a man as I've ever known. But he
was not a Seventh-day Adventist. My mother would take
us kids to church. We had a little church school in that
church, and when my mother took my older brother to get
him started in school there, I went with her. I was only five

years old. It was a small school; there were only four or five kids in the room. I went over and sat down at one of the little desks. It felt good sitting there. I liked it. After a while, Mother said, "Come on, it's time for you to go home."

I said, "I want to stay."

The teacher said, "Let him stay. If he gets tired, I'll call you, and you can come and get him."

Let me tell you. I never got tired! I'll never forget my first-grade teacher, Mrs. Jenkins. She taught me to read and to write and to count. I didn't know any of those things when I went to school. I just ate it up; I loved it. That school was provided by the Seventh-day Adventist Church. The church provided that education for me. You and I and all the members are the church. There is no church without the people that it is made up of. The Seventh-day Adventist people provided that little school. And I thank the church for the education it gave me.

Harry Holder came to be our teacher when I was in the fourth grade. He probably had only one year of college when he became my teacher, but what a teacher he was! Later on, he was named *Life* magazine's teacher of the year when he was teaching in the public school system in Lubbock, Texas. He was fantastic, and I had him in the fourth grade. More than anything else, he taught me about Jesus. Harry was a really strong guy, the strongest man I had ever known in my life at that point. He was very athletic, a real man. But most of all, he was a Christian, and I hadn't seen that combination much as a kid. I grew up in a church with twenty-seven members, all of them ladies except for one man. I want to tell you that I thank God for Harry Holder. I thank this church for giving me that kind of inspiration.

Harry held a Week of Prayer, an adult Week of Prayer for the whole church—not one just for children. I went every night and listened to him preach. And on Thursday night, I couldn't hold back any longer. I went forward and gave my life to Jesus. I was nine years old, and I made the choice to be baptized. The next year the church school closed, and I went to public school. That baptism was a beginning for me, and I thank God for that baptism.

When I got into public school, I found that I enjoyed sports. Actually, I *loved* sports. I was on the track team and ran the one-hundred-yard dash. I wasn't the fastest on the one-hundred-yard dash. Later, I told my kids that I was only one second off the world record in the one-hundred-yard dash—and that is true. But you have to realize that in the one-hundred-yard dash, one second translates into at least ten yards. That's a long way! Track events are calculated in milliseconds. So my sons finally figured this out when they got older, and they said, "You weren't fast at all, were you, Dad?" One second off the world record is a long, long way.

One of the fastest runners in the school, in fact, one of the fastest in the state, was my friend Sonny Haley. One Halloween, Sonny and I went out trick-or-treating, and we ended up aggravating this one poor fellow. We would knock on his door and then hide. Over and over again. The last time we went up to knock on his door, he flung it open, holding a shotgun! I want to tell you that at the end of two blocks, I was a full block in front of Sonny Haley! The next day Sonny told the track coach, "We have the fastest man in the world on our track team. Just put someone at the starting line holding a shotgun, and he'll win every time!"

I loved sports; baseball, most of all. I was determined that

I was going to be a professional baseball player. Now, in our family, we kids had to go to church with either Mom or Dad until we were sixteen years old. That was the rule. Then we could make our own decision about whether to keep going to church or not. My older siblings had all pretty much quit going to church, particularly the Seventh-day Adventist Church, for some time.

I was about to go into high school. I had played football and baseball in junior high. I pitched and played first base in baseball and had played quarterback in football. I was really looking forward to playing sports in high school. One of my older brothers had been an all-state football player; another one had been an all-state baseball player. The coaches were waiting for another Gilley to come along, and I wanted to be that one. I was about fourteen years old. Then suddenly, we got word at our little church that Fordyce Detamore was coming to town to hold evangelistic meetings.

At that time, I'd never heard of Fordyce Detamore. I didn't know he was a prominent Adventist evangelist. He was coming to our little church because the big meetings he had scheduled had been canceled for some reason. Our pastor had been a classmate of Elder Detamore and talked him into coming to our little church in Tyler, Texas, and hold meetings. Our pastor didn't tell him that there only twenty-seven members in our church!

When Elder Detamore arrived in Tyler, he was shocked by how small our church was. He preached that Sabbath morning, and he ripped us up! He gave it to us straight! "Look at that piano over there!" he said. "It looks like Noah's wife must have played it on the ark!" (Our piano was old and dilapidated.) "This place is filthy," he told us. "Look at all this stuff, stashed underneath the pulpit." And he started dragging out old pamphlets and Ingathering cans and old bulletins. "There is enough dust on that window sill to raise a crop!"

I liked Elder Detamore immediately. He didn't pull any punches. But I told my mother, "I'm not going to go to these meetings, Mother. I don't have the time. We're in the playoffs right now. Every night, we've got to either practice or play."

Now my mother was pretty gentle, but she could get strong when she needed to. She was desperate. She said, "Jim, you *are* going to these meetings—every night!"

"No, Mother. I'm not."

"Yes, you are!"

"What about the nights when I have a game?" I asked.

"If you have a game, you can go play. But you tell the coach that I said you couldn't be there for practice nights. On practice nights, you're going to be here for the meetings."

Then Mother made me an offer. She said, "If you attend all these meetings and if at the end you still don't want to be a Seventh-day Adventist, I'll accept that. You won't have to go to church anymore."

Wow! I thought. *I can cut two years off of having to go to church just by going to three weeks of meetings every night. That's a pretty good deal.*

"Are you sure about that?" I asked her.

"Yes. I'm sure."

So on the opening night of the meetings, I was there. Elder Detamore was an unbelievable preacher. He would race up and down the platform, back and forth, as he preached. They didn't have wireless microphones in those days. He had a lapel mic with a *long* cord. Ray Turner, his singing evangelist, would sit on the platform and reel Elder Detamore out and then reel him back in again as he paced back and forth across the platform. One little kid saw that cord and asked, "Mom, does that man run on electricity?"

I still remember the title of his sermon that opening night—"Our Shattered World." Elder Detamore talked about the political world and how it was shattered. He talked about how the family was shattered. He talked about how the financial world was shattered. He talked about how Christ was the only answer for our shattered world. As I listened to his message that night, it was the first time in my life that a preacher ever really reached my heart.

At the close of the sermon, Ray Turner sang "Deep River." Oh, it was beautiful! Roger Holley was with the team, as well. He conducted the song service. That night when the meeting was over and I walked outside the tent, my brother and two of my friends were there. They looked at me and said, "We're going to be preachers! What about you?"

I said, "No way! I'm going to be a professional baseball player." But deep down in my heart, I knew that somewhere, sometime, somehow, I'd be preaching this message. I knew it that night, and that was the first time I ever knew it. My brother and those two friends didn't end up becoming preachers, but those meetings affected their lives. Two of them are strong members of the church today. The third moved away, and I lost contact with him.

I'm so thankful that Elder Detamore came to our little church in Tyler and held those meetings! The church sent him, and I'm thankful to the church. I'm thankful to the members of this church—all of you who are working together to send this message around the world. It took one hundred years for the church to reach its first million members. That happened around 1960. Then we reached the second million and the third and the fourth. The latest statistical report put the world membership of the Seventh-day Adventist Church at 20.7 million as of the close of 2017! The Lord is pouring out His Spirit. I thank God for the fact that Adventists are spread all over the world, and I'm thankful for the church organization we have. You and I are part of something great, and I thank God for letting me be a part of it.

We don't always know how God has used us to touch other lives. But God knows. He can trace all the influences of your life on the lives of others. He knows the results of a word you have spoken—a kind deed, some money you have given. He knows what these things have done and the impact they have had. I think one of the joys of heaven will be finding out just how far-reaching our witness and influence have actually been. And I'm thankful God allows us to be a part of that.

When I left Tyler, Roger Holley came to our house and told my mother, "You have to get your boys into a Christian school."

"We don't have a church school here," she said.

Now, my father at the time was working in Dallas—staying there through the week and coming home on weekends. So Elder Holley told my mother, "Your husband is living in Dallas through the week. You need to move to Dallas with your husband."

"Oh, Dallas is a wicked city, Elder Holley!"

"Yes, it is," he agreed.

"And Tyler is a good city."

"Yes, it is," he agreed.

"So why should I move my boys to a wicked city?" my mother wanted to know.

And Elder Holley said, "Well, let me explain it to you this way. Tyler is a good city with no Christian education right now. And Dallas is a wicked city with a good church school. Dallas is where the boys' father is five days out of the week. Sister Gilley, I think you need to move these boys to Dallas, or you are going to lose them. You're going to lose them to the world if you stay here. They've made decisions to follow the Lord, but after we leave town, it's going to be difficult."

This conversation took place in August. Labor Day weekend, we loaded up our belongings and moved everything we had to Dallas in pickup load after pickup load. We moved into a rented house in a neighborhood that had a junior high school right down the street—I had one more year of junior high. I went down the street and watched the school's football team working out. I saw what they had for a quarterback, and I knew I could unseat that guy and take his place in three or four days. I wasn't being cocky, but I *knew* I could be the quarterback on that team. I guarantee you I could have done it.

I went home and told my dad, "I don't want to go to that church school. I want to play football at the junior high down the street."

Now my dad took glory in his sons playing ball; he loved that. So he said, "All right, you want to go to school there? You can."

I liked the sound of that! I got ready to enroll in school. My mother and my brother and I got in the car. My brother was going to enroll in church school. I said, "Mother, drop me off at the junior high first because I've got to be sure that I'm in seventh-period PE. If I'm not signed up for seventh-period PE, I can't be on the football team. They only let so many guys sign up for the seventh period, and I've got to be one of them."

She said, "No, I'm going to take your brother to enroll in church school first."

Now, my mother could be pretty stubborn, and she was driving. I started kicking up a storm!

She said, "Please, won't you go to church school?"

"No. I'm going to play football."

She said, "You can play ball in the summer."

I did play pony league baseball in the summer. I said, "Mother, I want to play football, and you can't play football in the summer."

"Playing ball doesn't have to be your whole life," she argued. She's preaching to me, and you know moms can preach pretty good. My mother could really preach, but I kept saying no.

Then she did something that's hard on a boy. She started crying. The tears were flowing down her face! And then she did something completely unfair. She pulled the car over to the curb, and she started praying for me—out loud!

I said, "Mother, you aren't going to change my mind. I love you, but I can play football and still serve the Lord." I was having a struggle, but I kept saying, "You're not going to change me. You're not going to change me. I won't turn away from the Lord."

We got over to the church school—Dallas Junior Academy— and she took my brother in while I stayed out in the car. Now you know how hot it gets in Texas in a car. I'm sitting there just as hot as I can be, and pretty soon, the principal comes out. He said, "You know we would really like to have you go to school here."

I said, "I'm not interested at all, but do you have any water in there?" I was thirsty.

"Yes," he said, "we have some water. Come on in."

So I went into the school and got a long drink at the water fountain. There were some kids in there, and they were letting loose. You see, the principal was also their teacher, and he was somewhere else enrolling my brother in school, so they were having a great time. I looked at them and said to myself, *That's a pretty good bunch of kids there. I think I might get along with them pretty good.*

I turned to leave, and it just hit me: *If you walk out this door, life's going to be different for you; it's going to be different. You're getting ready to make a mistake. Don't do it. Don't do it.* So I walked into the principal's office and said, "Go ahead and enroll me. I'm going to stay here."

And I did, and I thank God for that decision. I thank the Adventist Church for having this education system. You see, I'm an evangelist, and I believe in holding meetings and meetings and meetings. Whether you baptize one person or whether you baptize a thousand, I say, "Preach the gospel. Sow the seed. Do the work of an evangelist and leave the results to God." I believe in every aspect of the church, I believe in our schools. I believe that God has placed His blessing on everything we are doing. This message is moving forward, and I want to be a part of it. I thank God for all He has done in His church and my life. I thank the church for presenting Jesus to me and for presenting *all* the truth of Jesus, not just a portion.

I know that the church isn't perfect. It never has been, and it won't be until the Lord comes. The church wasn't perfect even in New Testament times. The church had imperfect people in it then—there were James and Peter. And the church has imperfect people in it today. But Jesus loves the church and gave Himself for it (Ephesians 5:25). If Jesus loves the church, then I have to love it, too, even if it's imperfect. If there were only perfect people in the church, then I wouldn't be able to be a part of it.

The apostle Paul tells us, "In everything give thanks; for this is the will of God in Christ Jesus for you" (1 Thessalonians 5:18). I'm so thankful to be a part of God's church! When I look back over my life and see the way the Lord has led, I'm thankful that He took an interest in me and guided me at crucial times when my life could have taken a much different direction. Ellen White could have been looking at my life when she wrote: "He [God] never leads them [His children] otherwise than they would choose to be led if they could see the end from the beginning, and discern the glory of the purpose that they are fulfilling."[1]

We need to cultivate an attitude of thankfulness. God has done great things for us; let's thank Him. Won't you spend some time today reflecting on all that the Lord has done for you and the way He has guided in your life—and say, "Thank You, Lord"? Follow the counsel of the psalmist: "Give thanks to the LORD, for He is good! For His mercy endures forever" (Psalm 106:1).

---

1. Ellen G. White, *Patriarchs and Prophets* (Mountain View, CA: Pacific Press®, 1942), 578.